Bob –

I know you ____
life will lead y___
real artisan for change. Good
luck on the changes ahead.

Tom H___

CHECKLIST
FOR
CHANGE

✔ CHECKLIST FOR CHANGE

A Pragmatic Approach to Creating and Controlling Change

THOMAS R. HARVEY
University of La Verne
Edited by Lillian B. Wehmeyer

Allyn and Bacon
Boston   London   Toronto   Sydney
Tokyo   Singapore

Library of Congress Cataloging-in-Publication Data

Harvey, Thomas R.
    Checklist for change : a pragmatic approach to creating and
controlling change / Thomas R. Harvey ; edited by Lillian B.
Wehmeyer.
            p.   cm.
    Includes bibliographical references.
    ISBN 0-205-12384-8
    1. Organizational change—Management. I. Wehmeyer, Lillian
Biermann, 1933–   . II. Title.
HD58.8.H375   1990
658.4'063–dc20   90-30178
                                                  CIP

Printed in the United States of America

10 9 8 7 6 5 4 3 2 1 94 93 92 91 90

To John and Scott,
who have more years to create change than I,
and more heart than most.

 # Contents

vii

✔ List of Figures and Forms

✔ FIGURES

✔ FORMS